All That Was Wood

i.m. Christian Brown

All That Was Wood
Poems from Cornerstone

Katherine Stansfield

SEREN

Seren is the book imprint of
Poetry Wales Press Ltd.
57 Nolton Street, Bridgend, Wales, CF31 3AE

www.serenbooks.com
facebook.com/SerenBooks
twitter@SerenBooks

The right of Katherine Stansfield to be identified as
the author of this work has been asserted in accordance
with the Copyright, Designs and Patents Act, 1988.

© Katherine Stansfield 2019.
Reprinted 2019.

ISBN: 978-1-78172-553-5

A CIP record for this title is available from the British Library.

All rights reserved. No part of this publication may be reproduced,
stored in a retrieval system, or transmitted at any time or by any means,
electronic, mechanical, photocopying, recording or otherwise without
the prior permission of the copyright holder.

The publisher acknowledges the financial assistance of the Welsh Books Council.

Printed in Bembo by 4Edge Ltd, Hockley.

Twitter: @K_Stansfield
www.katherinestansfield.blogspot.com

Contents

7	Mover & shaker
8	Prayer for protection
9	Watercourse
10	Watching *Godspell*
12	Proof for the policy-makers
13	Re-dedication
14	Telling the bees
15	*Notes on the poems*
16	*Author's note*

Mover & shaker

On bad days you think
you're going nowhere now,
you're *settled*
as a mountain, as a church,
as poems, all of which
can shift, of course.

I'm here to remind you of the zing
in your stones, how you're clad
in ballast shipped
to Cardiff from all the world
that took in coal – such travel
in your bones.

And what about those circus stars
sprung from your wooden floor
as if it was a trampoline?

You can't forget the discos.
Teenage lust left a charge
that zips between
hand dryers in the ladies' loos.
I've felt it. I know
the power of that crackly yearn.

And when I'm still
as the struts and eaves
in your hall, your heart,
I'm telling you you're anything
but static. Great stately
soul, great Cornerstone,

your history's long
for jiving.

Prayer for protection

Let the building be a shell
for the hermit crabs of faith.

Let the walls be sponges
soaked in all their prayers.

Let the sanctuary be just that
for those who need its love.

Let the vaulted roof keep safe
the stories of the church.

Let the window be the glass
to see their different views.

Let the table be the same
for all who want a seat.

Let them remember *this* is where
we learn such beautiful things.

Watercourse

In the storms we opened doors on either side,
stood clear for the flood to find its own expulsion
from the vestry

as is water's wont, like the women
who went in one door on their father's arm
and out the other on their husband's.

Saturday shoppers stopped to watch
this cuckoo clock
of newly-weds, as is their wont.

And the clock ticked on
and all the while the water that the flood had left
glistened

in the bricks, soon to desiccate
the mortar. Our baptisms were wetter
than was meant. All that was wood

bloomed mould, grew soft.
When the doors swelled shut I knew
our days were numbered

so I got to work. By the time
we handed back the keys I'd pulled away
a softened clump of wall:

my want. This damp is testament to who
I am, we are, this place–
I know it doesn't matter

where we go as long
as we're together
                          yet
I know

          my need:
that I'll
    be called

home swimming

Watching *Godspell*

Jesus, he's a looker, but it's John the Baptist's
satin top I have my eye on.

[FLASHBACK]:
                    John, he rocked up
in a knitted poncho, came amongst us
with cut-up Christmas paper blessings
scattered in the aisles.
                    For a while he was all
a prophet should be –

[CHORUS]:
                O Pharisees, o Hypocrites,
listen to your friend Jesus Christ. He just wants
to help you out with these skit-parables

[NOTES]:
            and that lovely swoopy fringe.

[FLASHBACK CONT'D]:

Day by day, the glitzy stories came. If I had ears
I was to listen: the Good Samaritan in leg warmers,
the disco lights of Lazarus.

[NOTES]:
            This could be done on roller skates.

[CHORUS]:
                    But then John, he took on
strange, and the lights went red, and this lovely young Jesus,
he said,
    '*One of you will betray me,*'
                            and that's when John,
he whipped off his poncho

[CUT TO SCENE]:
                    and *here's* the black satin number:
a close fit tunic – think Medieval executioner, Friday night –
with capped sleeves and a scalloped neck
                            for Judas
who was with us all along. We know how it goes from here.

[POSTSCRIPT]:
                    I find the tinsely-slips
of Christmas paper all the long days after –
in my coat, my slippers. Such glitter
                    is good for the soul.

Proof for the policy-makers

In Pontcanna the guitarist finished
his gig and a resident thanked him, said
You took from me all my troubles.
This was the first miracle.

The second was in Tremorfa
where a man who hadn't lifted
his head in years lindy-hopped
when the jazz band lit up.
The woman witness to this ran
weeping from the day room.

The miracles multiply:

from Newport, reports the tablet cups
are lighter. No repeat rattle-refrains
now that opera stars serve
arias with lunch.

In the Heath, lullabies for little ones
gone so long from their bedrooms
their old lives seem to belong
to strangers in the hospital's book
of bedtime stories. The singers are said
to bring blessings of sleep, kind dreams.

A few wards over, the harpist arrives
in the ICU, where the trolley
cacophony and anxious bass
of vital signs never cease. No relief
from the lights
                but the harpist
can look in the eye those who live flat,
those rehearsing their ends.

She plucks, and blood sings
while Death leaves them humming.

Re-dedication

Down Charles Street in the joy of bells
a century since this sound
tolled peace, but poorly then:
for the loss of hands
to pull the ropes, the Armistice
was patchy in its proclamation.

This morning the cathedral's brash
with noise – a din
to make believe the future
can be safer than the past,
as the flocks come back to Cornerstone
from all God's houses hereabouts.

We are witnesses to revenants:
a square of wood,
a pair of names.
The men who bore them
unreturned
but some losses, still,
can be undone.

Telling the bees

I'm here to tell the bees
in the garden you seeded
you've gone.

Since your passing
everything has bloomed –
bare earth reborn

oasis in this hectic
crook of M&S and Next,
shades of yellow and blue so

alive with light they warm
the darkness of the blind,
and I see the bees

knew before me, have gifted
us bright glory in our grief,
like this tenacious plant

by my side: the Six Hills' Giant
that can't be tamed. Cut back
it will return, beloved

by bees. In their kind hum
I hear again our meeting
on the stairs between poetry

last February:
not rushing off? you said.
Buck up, the bees tell me.

They have plans, I poems:
roots in this soil now.
Who knows what we can grow?

Notes on the poems

'Proof for the policy-makers'
Christian Brown was a great supporter of the charity Music in Hospitals and Care whose aim is to 'overcome barriers which prevent people, regardless of their health or well-being, from accessing the benefits of live music'. During my residency, Cornerstone hosted a breakfast meeting for those involved in the charity and I was able to learn about the fantastic work of MiHC in Wales.

For more information about Music in Hospitals and Care, and to make a donation to help their work, see https://mihc.org.uk/

'Watercourse'
I am extremely grateful to Petra Bennett of Eglwys Annibynnol Ebeneser for sharing her memories of the building which inform this poem (and for her meticulous help ensuring I had the story of Ebeneser right).

'Re-dedication'
On Sunday 11th November 2018, the centenary of the Armistice that marked the end of the First World War, a memorial service and dedication was held at Cornerstone. A plaque commemorating two members of the Charles Street Congregational Church who fell in the 1939-45 war, Willy Gotaas and Bernard Somerford, was returned to its original site beneath the First World War memorial window. The plaque had been removed from Charles St when members voted to join the United Reformed Church and merged with the Windsor Place English Presbyterian Church, now known as City United Reformed Church, Windsor Place.

The poem draws on an article that appeared in *The Observer* on 12th August 2018 entitled 'Plea for Bells to Toll Worldwide on War Centenary', and the words of Archbishop George Stack during the memorial service and dedication at Cornerstone.

My thanks to Alison Tansom for her help with the history of the Charles Street Congregational Church.

'Telling the bees'
The gardens at Cornerstone were developed in partnership with the Royal National Institute of Blind People, designed to facilitate disabled access and the needs of the Blind Gardening Club of Cardiff Institute for the Blind. The gardens have been planted to achieve highly visible contrasting colours, as well as distinctive scents.

Author's note

The building now known as Cornerstone opened in 1855 as the Charles Street Congregational Church. From 1978 to 2012 it was home to Eglwys Annibynnol Ebeneser (Ebeneser Independent Non-Conformist Church) and in 2012 the building was purchased by the Catholic Archdiocese of Cardiff. The Archdiocese secured a significant award from the Heritage Lottery Fund to renovate the building and transform it into the events space and community hub that is Cornerstone.

The project manager for the redevelopment was Christian Brown – a devotee of poetry amongst many other passions. Christian was instrumental in creating the Seren-Cornerstone Poetry Festival and after the inaugural event in 2018 he appointed me as Cornerstone's Poet in Residence for the following twelve months. My job was to attend a diverse range of events taking place in Cornerstone during that year and to write a pamphlet of new work in response. I was warmly welcomed by everyone I met and am grateful to all those who spoke with me, sang to me, shared with me.

Very sadly, Christian passed away suddenly in May 2018. I hope he would approve of these poems written during my tenure. He always seemed keen on the funny ones.

Thanks are due to the following people who have helped bring this pamphlet into being:

Lucy King at Cornerstone.

Amy Wack and all at Seren.

The sharp-eyed poets: Katy Birch, Mark Blayney, Emily Blewitt, Zillah Bowles, Kate North, clare e potter, Christina Thatcher, Hilary Watson, Susie Wild, Kate Wright.